EMPOWERMENT
IN THE
CLASSROOM

Simple and Practical Ideas to Make Teaching a Success for You and Your Students

DR. ARLENE KAISER

Empowerment in the Classroom

Arlene Kaiser, Ed.D., is a professional speaker, teacher and author. She presents keynote and workshop presentations throughout the United States and Canada for educational, business and non profit organizations. Some of her popular keynote presentations include: *Empowerment in the Workplace, Maintaining a Sense of Humor in Your Profession, Team Building, Presentation Skills, Effective Classroom Management, Parents and Teachers: Creating Diamonds and The Stages of Success or You Want Be Successful? Get a Horse!*

Arlene can be reached for scheduling a speaking engagement at (408) 946-4444.

Arlene Kaiser
Copyright © MCMXCVII

Cover design and text layout by Ad Graphics, Tulsa, Oklahoma 800 368-6196

Library of Congress Catalog Number: 97-074352

ISBN: 1-891221-00-0

Printed in the United States of America

What Others Are Saying About
Empowerment in the Classroom

"The three 'E's' in Arlene Kaiser's name stand for 'enthusiasm.' Arlene is Ms. Enthusiasm wherever she goes. She's got the formula. She can teach it to YOU. It's in her book. She has my enthusiastic affirmation. It's contagious with her."

Sidney B. Simon
Professor Emeritus, The University of Massachusetts
and author of *Getting Unstuck, IALAC* and
The Search For Values

"Arlene is the master of practical examples. She illustrates how teachers and students can empower each other to achieve success."

Jack Canfield
Inspirational Speaker and co-author
Chicken Soup for the Soul

"*Empowerment in the Classroom* is the perfect book to teach you how to understand students. Dr. Kaiser knows how to earn her students' trust. She knows the secrets to being a successful teacher and a friend to students. I know, Dr. Kaiser is my teacher."

Cheryl VanBeekom
8th grade student

"The enthusiasm and energy of Arlene Kaiser, combined with her dedication to her students, motivates students to do their best and not be afraid to "take a risk." She shares practical information in her book to empower educators."

Linda Weidner
Parent

"Arlene's wholehearted love of children, her enthusiasm for learning and teaching contributes to the success of this book. I can always learn from her."

Her mother
Marie Kaiser, R.N., MFCC

"Empowerment in the Classroom™" is a trademark of August Press, Arlene Kaiser Production and Arlene Kaiser, indicating a series of products that may include but is not limited to books, pocket cards, audio cassettes and video tapes.

Published by
August Press
Santa Clara County, California

Order Information
To order more copies of this book or to receive an order form of other products by Arlene Kaiser contact:

Arlene Kaiser Productions
by calling:

(408) 946-4444

Other Books Available
by
Arlene Kaiser

Squince the Unique Squirrel

11 Ways to Keep Your Enthusiasm for Teaching

First Aid for a Broken Heart

Green Light Christians

Special Thanks to:

Sherry Blackman, my editor, who kept me on track.

The administrators, teachers, students and others who have generously contributed to this book by their example, generosity, and encouragement.

Donald Cravalho, my former student who is an accomplished cartoonist and creatively contributed to this book.

David Granlund of Middlesex News, Framingham, Massachusetts, who graciously shared his delightful cartoon and inspired me with his generosity.

Goddard Sherman, a cartoonist and retired teacher, who shared his talent.

Jack Wilson, retired teacher, Presbyterian minister, cowboy poet, and most of all, my beloved husband. He encouraged me to write this book, and always enhances my self-esteem with his unconditional love.

Dedication

This book is dedicated to Marie M. Kaiser, my mother. You have always been my best supporter. Thank you for encouraging me to stick with teaching even when I wanted to quit after my first devastating year. I would have missed out on the greatest joy and challenge of a life time. Thank you for your profound love of education. It has rubbed off on me and enhanced my life. God bless you, Mom!

CONTENTS

Introduction

"A child is a person who is going to carry out what you have started. He is going to sit where you are sitting, and when you are gone, attend to those things that you think are important. You may adopt all the policies you please, but how they are carried out depends on him. He will assume control of your cities , states, and nations. He is going to move in and take over your churches, schools, universities, and corporations. The fate of humanity is in his hands."

Abraham Lincoln

As a professional speaker and educator, I have had the privilege to speak to teachers, administrators, and parents throughout the United States. I have taught at the elementary and secondary levels for over twenty years. As I publish this book, I am teaching in a public school.

I join the many educators who want to be effective and successful with students. I recognize we are a team: working, learning, and growing together to make a positive impact on the lives of our students. It is clear to me that if the teacher is empowered in the classroom, the students will be empowered to learn. We have a double responsibility to the students, to prepare them for the future while guiding them in the present.

As a successful teacher, I continue to learn from my colleagues and strive to apply new ideas and strategies to my own classroom. Many of these ideas, to the delight of my students, have empowered me as a teacher. While presenting keynote and workshop presentations, participants have asked me to put the ideas I discuss in book form. Throughout the writing of this book I have been keenly aware of the words of Galileo. "You cannot teach a man anything you can only help him discover it within himself." May you discover at least one idea to spark the creativity within you and empower you in your classroom and school.

May I suggest that you relax and read through this book in one sitting. I did not write a voluminous book, but a book which can be easily read and passed on to another educator. After an initial reading, you can always go back and apply the ideas to your own situation and your unique style of teaching. My purpose in writing this book is threefold: to give the new teacher ideas and encouragement, the veteran teacher validation and perspective and the administrator insight and encouragement. May we never forget that "Inspiration from a teacher can last a lifetime."

Paying My Dues

It was the early 1970s. I was ready to begin my teaching career. I knew all there was to know about teaching: in one hand I had my elementary and secondary teaching credentials, in the other hand, I had the experience of student teaching in a fourth and a seventh grade class. However, because of an abundance of teachers in California it was difficult to get a teaching position. In desperation, I became a substitute teacher, hopeful that it would open the door to a permanent position.

The month was February. Early one morning the call came for me to substitute in a sixth grade class. With excitement and apprehension I accepted the assignment. I should have known something was wrong when I arrived at the school office. Without even greeting me or looking up, the secretary asked who I was. I responded cheerfully, "I'm the substitute for the sixth grade class." She tossed the classroom key in my direction and pointed her bony finger toward the long dark hallway. As I walked down the hall two teachers opened their doors asking if I was lost. I explained I was substituting for Mrs. J. They looked at each other, shook their heads, rolled their eyes to the ceiling as if they were saying, "Not again!" and closed their doors slowly behind them. Now I am not a superstitious person, but I was jarred when I found the classroom with the number 13 just above the door. As I put my hand on the door knob the door flung open. A trembling woman, with tears streaming down her face, sobbed, "Maybe you can do something with them!" And she rushed past me. I slowly stepped into the classroom. I scanned the 32 sixth graders. They were silent and carefully scrutinizing me. A boy slowly rose to his feet. Next to my 5'2" frame he appeared to stand at least 15 or 20 feet tall. He peered down at me and snarled, "You wanna see what we did to get rid of the other teachers?" The class had forced two teachers to resign and I was the third substitute teacher. I became the final long term substitute and taught, no, barely survived, until June. Each evening from 7:00 until 10:00 I graded papers, redesigned lesson plans, scheduled free time and then cried myself to sleep dreading the next day at school.

The experience of that class nearly caused me to quit the teaching profession. The only reason I stayed was because of the encouragement of others. Veteran teachers assured me that not all classes were this bad. Others cautioned me to remain so I would have the opportunity for a permanent teaching position with a different group of students.

It has been many years since that sixth grade ordeal. To date, it was the most miserable teaching experience of my life and I have never come close to a repeat performance.

Have you had a similar experience? Perhaps you have a class like that now! Maybe you are so discouraged you are ready to leave the teaching profession. Or, to date, you have been fortunate to never have had such an experience. Whatever your situation I bring you ideas, and wisdom from my classroom as well as the classrooms of other successful teachers. These strategies, ideas and concepts work to make teaching a joy for you and a positive learning environment for students. I am not presumptuous enough to think that all teachers should teach my way, or use all of these ideas in the student and teacher relationship and classroom management. The information in this book is like a smorgasbord. Freely take that what will work with your own style of teaching or management of a school. Happy reading!

"You wanna see what we did to get rid of the other teachers?"

Road Signs to Success

On a return drive from Reno, Nevada to the Bay Area, I was intrigued by the many road signs posted for the many truckers traveling through the Sierra Mountains on Highway 80. "Let her drift, crank her up, 6% grade ahead, advise 45 MPH." Throughout the varying grades were signs coaching the truck drivers. It occurred to me that another trucker had tested the roadway. He/she had evaluated the road then decided what would help other truckers to be safe in their drive down the steep mountain. Wouldn't it be a help to have road signs posted along the pathway of life. That's what we do as teachers. We were once students and we traveled the educational road just as our students. We have experienced exciting classrooms and some of us have been damaged by ineffective teachers. Let's readily share our road signs with students. They may not always seem to pay attention but don't surprised at what they will learn from our experience. What road signs would you post along the pathway of life?

Road Signs to Success

Classroom Management

As a beginning teacher I wanted the students to like me. I wanted to be one of their favorites. I thought if they liked me, and we were friends, then we would work successfully together. We would have productive discussions, they would complete their homework and the discipline problems would be few. Fortunately, I listened to a wise educator of 35 years, my mother, when she told me the following story.

Imagine you are interested in learning to paddle a canoe down a large turbulent river. After some lessons, you are ready to enter the water. You would not immediately paddle out into the middle of the river where the current is swift. You would stay close to the edge of the shore until you gain confidence in your mobility through the water. Once you master those canoeing techniques, you might paddle confidently to the other side of the river or careen down the middle through the rapids. Whenever you lost control, you would return to the edge of the shore where the water is calm. That's how it is with classroom management.

The first day of class is not the time to let the students do whatever they want to do. It is not the time for the teacher to sit back and relax and let them guess the structure and routine of their class.

Stay close to shore: be the Chief Executive Officer of the classroom. Give students clear expectations. Have them rehearse your classroom procedures. Through this process of rehearsing and learning the boundaries you will be able to spot if and when you are losing control. Someone needs to be in charge! As the teacher you are expected to be the CEO.

Children need and appreciate routine. They need to know what is expected and what are the cues for changing from one activity to another. A byproduct of being a good classroom manager and treating students fairly is that students return your respect. Not surprisingly their respect often becomes admiration, and appreciation! However, this is not the focus. You are not in this profession to be the students' buddy. They have buddies. They need a teacher! There is a big difference.

Connecting/Belonging: The Team Approach

The team approach, people working together for the successful completion of a common goal, project or product, is still valid in business organizations. In successful families there is a team approach which creates a sense of belonging. But unfortunately due to the pressures of work and unstable family situations the team is often weak or dysfunctional. As educators we find ourselves a catalyst for building that sense of belonging in our students which comes from being on a team. Is it really of such great importance? You bet it is!

One of the great joys of being a human is receiving and giving support and understanding from others. I often test my many theories about students and all human beings. One such experiment was especially delightful. My husband I made a purchase in a souvenir store. Upon paying for the item

I saw that I needed a penny. Now I had a dime but I didn't want all those pennies returned as change so I just blurted enthusiastically. "Does anybody have a penny I could have?" It was surprising to see that about six people came to my rescue reaching in their pockets and purses to give me that penny. I bet you would have reached in your pocket to help. There is nothing like connecting with others especially during difficult times.

I remember two more serious instances. First, I stood with my parents as we watched their house burn. Neighbors reached out to support us with food, clothing, and especially emotional support. Secondly, during the hospital stay and finally the death of my father we were supported by complete strangers. People waiting in the hospital for their loved ones shared encouraging words, a postal clerk ushered me to the font of the line so I could return to the hospital, a bank teller who graciously filled out my deposit slip while tears blurred my vision.

Regularly, I see students comforting each other. It may be the breakup of a relationship, or the news of their parents divorce, or the loss of a pet. We need to give more opportunities for our students to build those connections and that sense of belonging. This need for connection and its positive results wont end at school, it spills over into society improving the world at large.

Begin at the Beginning

It's almost the start of the school year or the beginning of your teaching semester. You know it's close because you have those wacky nightmares... you know, the ones where you try to gain control of your class but no sound comes from your throat. Or the nightmare where you can't find your classroom? Whatever the nightmare, most of us have had them. Perhaps we have them because we are anxious about the incoming students. We speculate about the first few weeks of school and our effectiveness in the classroom. Which brings me to the question. What do you want your classroom to look like? I don't mean the bulletin boards, posters, or colorful boarder around the blackboard. I mean what is the atmosphere? What kind of activities occur and how do you switch from one activity to another? What is the emotional environment of the classroom, how do you treat students and how do they treat you? Develop a clear mental picture of what you want your classroom to look, sound and feel like.

The first two weeks of school I use to "rehearse" appropriate classroom procedures. I relate much of what I teach to life skills. For example, if a student was going to work he would have signed a contract, be informed about hours of work, breaks, holidays, sick leave, and where to go for assistance. There would be a performance review. Also some of the task required would not necessarily be met with enthusiasm. There are aspects of work that may not be fun to do, but they need to be completed. It is part of the job!

Create A Contract

In my classroom each student has a contract, which is given the first week of school. As a group we go over the contract word for word. Also, I have their parents read and sign the contract. The students sign it in autograph style (they love this) and then print their name so I can read it. I have never had a student or parent refuse to sign a contract. I keep the contract until the last day of school. It is returned with *Job Completed* stamped on it. The contract illustrated is not meant to be copied word

CLASS CONTRACT

As a student of (*name of school*) and a member of (*name of teacher and class*), I do agree to the following:

1. I will raise my hand before I speak, and I will act as if I am interested. Even if I get bored and want to do something else, I will act as if I am extremely interested in what is going on in the class.

2. I will complete my homework and follow classroom procedures and expectations as explained in the handout.

3. During group work I will act as a responsible and trustworthy student. I will work independently as well as with other students. I may not like all the people with whom I work but I will respect them as fellow students and their right to learn in this classroom.

4. I will practice the great skill of listening...especially when (name of the teacher) is demonstrating or lecturing.

5. As a student desiring to be above average, I will be an outstanding class member. I will listen and applaud my fellow students when appropriate.

6. Great courage is necessary in this class, therefore, I will not say, "I don't know" to questions from the teacher. As I have a creative mind I will at least make-up an answer.

7. I will take the risk to enjoy myself, to build my self-esteem and the esteem of others.

8. If I do not fulfill this contract, I understand the following consequences will occur:
    1. A warning from the teacher
    2. A private talk during class with the teacher in the hall
    3. A call to my parents at home or at their work
    4. A Vice Principal referral
    5. A class suspension for one or two days

9. If I do fulfill this contract I understand the following benefits are available:
    1. Working in a stress free environment.
    2. The privilege of working with my friends.
    3. Opportunity to invite my friends from other classes to view my work and share in the celebration of a project completed.
    4. Opportunity to attend field trips and enjoy class free time.
    5. To receive the validation and appreciation of my teacher.
    6. To successfully complete the requirement of this class.

This agreement is signed by _____

Print your name: _____

Grade: _____

Parent signature: _____

Today's date:_____(Teacher's Signature)_____

for word. It is effective in my classroom because it has been designed for my students' as well as my needs. You know your students. Over the years I have adapted the contract to what works. With the younger ages the contract would be greatly simplified yet it can still be useful. Remember, this is a smorgasbord. Use what you like and discard the rest.

Explanation of the Contract

1. I will raise my hand before I speak, and I will act as if I am interested. Even if I get bored and want to do something else, I will act as if I am extremely interested in what is going on in the class.

Getting students to raise their hands before they speak can be a continuous battle. Also, it can be frustrating to see students rolling their eyes, yawning loudly, getting up to get a drink or sharpening their pencils in the middle of a lecture or a presentation by other students. This is not appropriate behavior and students often do not know what is appropriate and what isn't. No one has taught them. Also, if they aren't interested, at least pretend! Act as if. I often demonstrate what "acting like I am extremely interested" looks like: sitting up straight, leaning forward, eye contact and taking notes. Surely this is a social skill that will enhance their interpersonal relationships whether at school or in a working environment.

2. I will complete my homework and follow classroom procedures and expectations as explained in the handout.

Wouldn't it be wonderful to have students complete their homework every single day? My experience tells me the number one reason a student fails a class is not completing their homework. They tell their parents they don't have any homework or they already did it at school. Completing homework is a continuous challenge. As an adult, I still find it difficult to complete my own "homework" such as filing income tax on time, mailing bills, completing class lesson plans, or remembering family events and special occasions. Homework is difficult for most of us. Because it continues throughout life however, teachers can never stop demanding that they "do their homework." However, I do believe there comes a time when we have done everything we can to encourage the student, but the choice is ultimately theirs! Sometimes they choose to fail a class by not doing their homework. It is unjust to allow them to slide by without fulfilling the requirements of the class. Again, look at business. If an employee continually fails to not carry his/her load that employee will be replaced. If a student chooses to go to college and not do the homework they will ultimately fail. Let's be consistent. There are painful consequences in life for not fulfilling requirements. Homework habits teach students how to attack this life long task.

To give students a clearer perspective on the "homework" issue I give the following assignment: "Ask your parents to list the 'homework' they have to do as adults." Each student returns to class, stands by their desk and reads his/her list. They see that adults also have "homework" and it isn't always fun. I also relate homework to paying bills. Students hope to one day drive their **own** car, have their **own** apartment, travel, and buy whatever they want at the mall. To do adult activities means they will have to pay their bills. Isn't homework like paying a bill? That is why I encourage students to turn something in, show me some effort was made to complete the assignment. Isn't this like making

some payment on an overdue account? Students
need to learn the habit of showing effort. The worst
they can do is to do nothing!

3. During group work I will act as a responsible
   and trustworthy student. I will work independently as well as with other students. I may not
   like all the people I work with but I will respect
   them as fellow students and their right to learn
   in this classroom.

Students need to learn responsibility and trust. We
need to give them the opportunity to exhibit this
behavior. In the future, they will not always work
with the people of their choice. In your work do you
get to select the people with whom you will work?
Students might as well practice the skill of creating
good human relations which will be needed in the
future. Since life involves people, this is another
skill they will always need.

4. I will practice the great skill of listening...especially
   when (name of the teacher) is demonstrating or
   lecturing.

You have a right to teach and students have a right
to learn. Students are depending on you to teach
them. It is frustrating and energy draining for any
teacher to lecture or demonstrate while students
continue chattering. This is not fair to the students.
They can learn to listen. They need to learn to listen.

5. As a student desiring to be above average I will
   be an outstanding class member. I will listen
   and applaud my fellow students when appropriate.

I realize that not every student entering class wants
to be an above average or an outstanding student.
Most students, however, want to succeed and have

24

the teacher like them. I include this as a teacher expectation. I expect them to do their best. Most of the time they meet the expectation. The skill of listening is not just for the teacher but for other students as well. Students need to give positive feedback to their peers. I have asked hundreds of employees, parents, teachers, and students, how many of them receive enough appreciation. At least 98% have acknowledged the need for more validation and appreciation. School is the perfect place to learn the skill of giving and receive validation and appreciation.

6. As I realize that great courage is necessary in this class, I will not say, "I don't know" to questions asked by the teacher. I have a creative mind and I will at least make-up an answer.

The age group I teach almost always answers any question with an "I don't know." The frustration is they often do know the correct answer. So, I just do not allow, "I don't know." I have observed teachers getting impatient when there is silence. Students often learn that if they just keep their mouths shut, smile, and are polite they won't be bothered and will probably pass the class. Not in my class! I will stick with them until they **say something!** For the very shy students I handle this with great support and gentleness. I will not move on to another student whom I know has the correct answer. It doesn't do any good for the other students to wave their hands, snap their fingers and say, "I know, I know." I will stick with the shy student until something is said. If the student doesn't get the correct answer, I'll tell him/her it's not correct but what great work he/she did in **taking the risk** to create an answer to the question. That student knows I am proud. As students progress through the semester confidence increases and the frozen hands are enthusiastically raised to answer questions.

7. I will take the risk to enjoy myself, to build my self-esteem and the esteem of others.

Students need to be encouraged to take risks and to speak positively of themselves as well as others. Yes, many of the activities can and should be enjoyed. School doesn't have to be all drudgery. We can laugh and enjoy each other. I often feel the closest to my students when we have a great laugh together. It is energizing and healthy!

8. If I do not fulfill this contract, I understand the following consequences will occur:

   1. A warning from the teacher
   2. A private talk during class with the teacher in the hall
   3. A call to my parents at home or at their work
   4. A Vice Principal referral
   5. A class suspension for one or two days

As stated earlier, misbehavior is not good for students. They need clear consequences for their choice of actions. The warning I give is a calm verbal "warning." I have very few vice principal referrals. The classroom suspensions are rare. However, I will use them if needed and first contact the parent. As the CEO of the classroom I need to manage the discipline problems. The vice principal is my support system and in serious situations when I have exhausted my resources I will not hesitate to refer students to the office.

Having worked as a vice principal I was astounded at the situations referred to the office by teachers. The majority of behavior problems could and should have been handled by the classroom CEO. This contract and keeping parents informed have decreased the discipline problems in my classroom. The expectation that I will have cooperative students usually comes true!

9. If I do fulfill this contract I understand the following benefits are available:

    1. Working in a stress free environment.

    2. The privilege to work with my friends.

    3. Opportunity to invite my friends from other classes to view my work and share in the celebration of work completed.

    4. Opportunity to attend field trips and enjoy class free time.

    5. To receive the validation and appreciation of my teacher.

    6. To successfully complete the requirements of this class.

This is the best part of the contract. As I relate so much of student behavior to the business world I am reminded of the benefits, rewards, celebrations, and bonuses valued employees receive. Now, I can't allow my students to leave school early. They would like to. I do not pay them wages. They would love to get paid. I do not give them gifts. They would love to get presents. But there are so many wonderful ways to show my appreciation for their cooperation and a job well done. First, they attend a class that is exciting, safe, fun and challenging. Second, I ask for their input as to suggestions as to how they would like to celebrate their success. The most popular celebration is the pizza party for the classes that receive A's for their cooperation with the substitute teacher for the days I am absent during the semester. Usually I end up buying lots of pizza for all my classes. Such a small price to pay to reinforce the value of good work ethics and working together for a common goal, pizza. Substitute teachers eagerly take my class and I am at peace knowing that the students will treat the interim CEO with the same respect I receive. Most of the benefits for their cooperation are selected by the students. Past benefits for cooperation have included: donuts, taking their desk outside into the sunshine and working with their friends, video taping assignments and inviting their friends from other classes to see their performance and enjoying popcorn, listening to their music (always evaluated carefully by another student so I don't lose my job) rather than my elevator music, going to the library to finish homework for another class, and enjoying field trips together. The students ask for so little. They really just want to be liked and appreciated by the teacher! They <u>want you</u> to like them.

What would you put in your contract? If you are a new teacher seek out ideas from your colleagues. As a veteran teacher reflect on your past years of teaching. Is there anything you would like to change? Other ideas include: evaluate what gives you energy from your students and what depletes your enthusiasm, compare contracts used in business with your ideas. If you have never used a contract I encourage you to try it.

Create Classroom Procedures and Expectations

This is another form distributed the first two weeks of school. I explain and demonstrate some of the procedures. You will probably laugh at some of these. Many of the procedures have to do with giving me energy rather than depleting my enthusiasm. For example, in the past when I would say, "Open your homework book for tonight's assignment." The students would moan and groan. I felt terrible, like

Dad, will you sign my contract for school?

I was the villain in a melodrama. Every day the same reaction to my homework announcement. One day, I decided to take a different approach. I explained to the students all the homework I had in preparation for their class, the years of homework I had to do to become a teacher. I told them honestly that I didn't like homework. I would much rather visit with my husband, go to a movie, ride my horse, read a book, but if I wanted to continue to be married, teach, own a home, a car, and spend money, I had homework or chores to complete. I further stated, "Since we all are in this together in having to do homework let's take some of the misery out of it. From now on, even though most of us don't mean it, even though most of us don't want to do it. When

I say, 'Open your homework books.' You are all to reply. 'I love to learn!' with enthusiasm! When you do this I will often reply, 'And I love to grade those papers.'" As a result of this routine we giggle together and they write down the homework, do the assignment and I correct those papers. That response of hearing 35 students say in unison, "I loooooove to learn!" zaps me with the greatest shot of energy. I don't feel like the villain any more. Five times a day I hear that united chorus. It empowers me in the classroom so I can empower the students to success.

Students really want to help. They want a peaceful yet structures classroom. They also want to look forward to your class. If you don't believe that talk with students near the end of summer. They can't wait to get back to school!

Ask or tell your students how they can contribute to energizing your teaching skills. But first ask yourself, "What gives me energy and what depletes my enthusiasm for teaching?" Your procedures will be different. Put them down in writing for all to see.

The Classroom Procedures and Expectations

Name _____ Grade _____

Period _____ Date _____

The classroom boundaries include around _Dr. Kaiser's desk_ and _green cabinet._

After Dr. Kaiser says, "Open up your homework books!" students are to say, _"I love to learn."_

Students are not allowed to use_ profanity _ and they may not say, _"I don't know"_ to any question Dr. Kaiser asks.

Audience etiquette means _ how you behave as an audience member._

As a member of the audience you may not use put downs _in your voice_ or_body actions._

CEO stands for _ Chief Executive Officer._

If you ask a question such as "What are we going to do today?" Dr. Kaiser will just look at you and smile. She will do this for any question that she will explain to the entire class.

She needs to conserve her _energy_ for her other classes.

Students have a right to _learn_ and Dr. Kaiser has a right to _teach._

If Students are inappropriate in their behavior Dr. Kaiser will first give a verbal _"warning."_

Next, she will speak to the person privately _in the hall._

Next, she will have the student call his/her parent.

For outstanding cooperation in class students may invite other _students_ from other classes to see their performance.

For this class to be a fun, exciting, and a learning experience the class must be built on _trust and responsibility._

The classroom pledge is like a _mission statement._

I Love To Learn

Open up your homework books

Classroom Organization

Everyone participates. Just like in a real job, someone makes the coffee, someone turns the lights out, completes paper work, locks the door, turns the computers off, deposits the money, etc. Not all tasks are fun, but all need to be done in order to stay in business. As I have interviewed business executives and employees they still tell me they are on the lookout for employees who are motivated, work well with others and show promise for advancement. In the classroom who is willing to help? Recently I had the privilege to speak at a middle school. Among guests attending was computer genius Steve Wozniak. I took the opportunity to meet and interview him. "What do I need to teach my students so that they can be effective in the work place?" I asked. After thoughtful consideration he answered, "Teach them to be helpful. To be helpful with others."

One of the ways to teach students to be helpful is for them to take responsibility for the smooth operation of the classroom. This entails assisting with classroom organization. Every week students sign up for a classroom assistant position. At the end of the week or the beginning of the next, the student will select another student to replace him/her in the assistant position. Students may not work in any position two consecutive weeks in a row. All students are expected to know all the job assignments and the responsibilities for that position. All students are expected to work during the semester. The frequency of their participation will be added to their "attitude grades" which are included with their academic and attendance grade. For someone who doesn't like paper work how do you keep track of all those students who have participated or not participated? Very simple. I keep all the chart papers for the nine week period, just posting the charts one on top of the other throughout the quarter. The last few days of the grading period I display them throughout the room. Each student counts up the number of times their name appears on the chart. Individually they tell me the number or with a randomly selected partner they tabulate each others' score and report the results. No, I do not meticulously check each and every student's score. If there is a student I have concern about, I check to see if the number matches mine. Since the entire class can see the scores there are very few mistakes. This can also be a job for the Classroom Teachers Assistant.

The Pledge/Messenger Person

The Pledge person begins the official start of class time. As soon as the tardy bell finishing ringing the pledge person takes center stage of the classroom. The pledge gets us focused on the class and ready to go to work. I don't start the class. The pledge person does. One period a day we do the flag pledge. The other classes only say the classroom pledge. The classroom pledge is really our mission statement. We say together," I am responsible for my own behavior. I will make quality choices all the time."

For this position the student needs to be shown how to appropriately ask the students to stand, then to wait patiently for all students to stand and then give a cue such as, "Ready begin." and to say after completion of the pledge, " You may be seated." This may seem so simple to adults but haven't you seen a student slouching, chewing gum, and mumbling while leading a pledge in the classroom or an assembly? I do not hesitate to correct the student and am willing to repeat the pledge until the task is performed correctly. Since most of the students are reluctant to get in front of the class as the pledge person I added **Messenger Person** to this assignment.

Everyone in the class likes to have the privilege of leaving the classroom to deliver a message to the office or to another classroom. By making this a two assignment position I always get students to volunteer. The messenger's responsibilities include how to deliver a message appropriately, and how to approach another class in session. I often get feedback from other teachers as to how well the student did in delivering a message. I have even been known to write a note sealed in an envelope passed on to a teacher or school secretary which says, "I just need to let this student have the privilege of delivering message. No need to answer just send the student back to class and give him lots of validation. He needs it today. Thanks," The faculty and staff I work with are so supportive. We are a team!

Telephone and Homework Assistant

Do you have a telephone in your room? If so, your students need to learn how to answer the telephone appropriately. Years ago I heard Zig Ziglar speak in his popular self-esteem course, *The I Can Class.* I took some of his concepts and applied them to my classroom. When the **Telephone Assistant** answers our class phone he/she will say, "Hello, we're having a great day in Dr. Kaiser's class, may I help you? The telephone assistant answers the phone this way whether he/she feels like it or not. Isn't it true they will have to answer a business phone with a cheerful company greeting? Students need to be shown how to respond to the request of the caller. When should the student interrupt the teacher, and what is an appropriate way to interrupt for a telephone call? When should a message be taken? This all has to be taught and rehearsed over and over. Parents especially appreciate this training which carries over to improve home telephone manners. Because most students like to answer the telephone, but not record the homework I added two jobs to one.

The homework responsibility of this position includes writing down the homework each day it is assigned. Sometimes in my creative moments I might alter an assignment. I rely on the homework person to write down the new assignment exactly as I have assigned it. Often you will hear me say, "Homework person, please read back the homework assignment for the class." It is also imperative that the homework person thoroughly understand the assignment; in the event someone is absent he/she can give the makeup assignment accurately.

The Recorder

There is information I need to have recorded. Examples are selection of partners or assigning of groups. Also, the assignment needs to be written down. The recorder writes down the names of the partners or group members and copies word for word the assignment I dictate for a particular group. The recorder's position is extremely valuable. Anytime in class I may say, "Recorder, repeat the names of the group members and their directions for the assignment due in two weeks" The student will

Classroom
organization,
everyone helps.

stand and read word for word what I dictated. Sometimes I don't even remember what I said! But the recorder does. The recorder may keep the assigned names and groups in his binder or I may ask to keep them in my plan book. There is some over lapping with the homework person but plenty of work for two positions.

Incidentally, I often have the students stand to answer questions, read a short paragraph, or respond as the recorder. They are shown how to stand. They do not slump across their desk, or slouch on one foot. They stand straight and tall even if they don't feel like it, even if they are embarrassed. With gentle encouragement and persistence they stand.

Students need the opportunity to practice thinking on their feet and standing with confidence and poise even if they don't feel like it. It my class they get that opportunity.

The Paper Distributor

I admit I do not like to do paper work. I just want to teach, not hand out and correct papers; however, as a professional I do the paper work. Anything I can do to make the paper work more manageable I am willing to do.

The Paper Distributor passes out all paper in an orderly fashion. Sometimes he/she needs an assistant to help and can select one or two of his/her friends to help. I merely say, "Paper Distributor," and miraculously he or she appears ready to pass out papers.

The Collector

I give a number to all of my students. The **Collector** gathers the papers that need to be graded, organizes the papers facing the same way, checks to see that the proper heading has been included with the assigned number. The papers are put in numerical order before giving them to me. This way I can quickly write the grades in the grade book as the student's name is listed in the same numerical order.

Teacher Assistant

I do not always use a teacher assistant. When I do it is because I need consistent help with paper work. This is a semester position. I announce to the class I am looking for a Teacher Assistant. The requirements include: an A in English, good attendance, trustworthiness, honesty, dependability, computer skills are appreciated. Parents permission and support is mandatory. If students are interested they complete an application and are interviewed by me. I contact their parents and see if they agree their child could faithfully execute the position. Since teacher assistants also complete classroom assignments this can be quite a load for some students and for others a welcomed challenge. The parents input is very helpful in making this decision.

The paperwork involved in teaching is insurmountable.

Substitute Teachers

For a year I was a substitute teacher for K -12 grades. In some classes I was treated with respect and in others with contempt. I also was welcomed by some faculty and treated as a colleague. In other schools, I was treated as "less than". So I have experienced both sides of the fence. I made a decision when I returned to teaching after six years in business, that I would not tolerate inappropriate behavior toward a substitute teacher. I would do all in my power to get a professional substitute in my class, however, in the event a substitute wasn't of my choosing the students still needed to treat him/ her as a guest CEO. Again, in business, management changes. Employees do not get to cast the final vote and select the new boss. The work needs to continue. The same is true in the classroom. I get so frustrated at teachers who say, "Oh, I can't leave the classroom to attend a seminar or conference, my students need me. They will miss out on teaching time." I say, "bologna!" They can learn with a substitute teacher! If the teacher has created good lesson plans, has an organized class, and high expectations the learning will occur. Having a substitute teacher can be a learning experience for the students and the regular classroom teacher! Naturally it takes more preparation on the part of the classroom teacher.

For the past ten years I have used substitutes regularly in my classroom. Sometimes I get to select the substitute and other times the school district will select the substitute teacher. Some are better than others; however, I still view them as guest CEO's to the classroom. At the beginning of school I prepare the students for a "guest teacher." My colleague, Liz Mertens, a former substitute teacher, gave me the idea to have the substitute teacher score each class for overall behavior. A chart is designed and left in the classroom. At the end of each period the substitute puts the rating of the entire class on the chart. The scores are 1 -10, with 10 being the top score. When I return with one quick glance, I can see how the class went. The scores, since I have used this system, have remained in the 9's and 10's. The lowest score the students chose to receive was a 5. The next five days I was out it remained a prefect 10. You might be thinking, "that's all fine and good for you but you don't know my students, they would never cooperate with a substitute." First, I do not believe my students are much different than yours. We probably could match case histories of students. So, let's dispel that myth. This is how the system works for me.

The first two weeks of school I announce that from time to time I will be out of the classroom. The students will have a substitute teacher. I expect the students to treat the sub just as they treat me. I then assign my students to ask their parents if they ever worked for a boss who celebrated the company's success with employees. Perhaps they got a longer lunch hour, donuts, a bonus, an extra day off. Anything, where they were shown and told, "job well done!" This does happen in the business world! Employees need validation just as students do. So, we discuss and brainstorm different ways we can celebrate the students' choice to cooperate with a substitute. In the past their list has included: listening to their music, working outside in the sunshine, having free time, skipping a homework assignment, seeing a class related video, a break to play basketball, getting an extra stamp on their ScoreCard, playing a game, working with a friend, and pizza. In reality, the students ask for so little. As the CEO I have the option to eliminate any of their ideas which might conflict with school rules or just be inappropriate. It seems that pizza is always a top request and so I do give a pizza lunch for the class or classes that get consecutive 10's for their behavior with a substitute. There have been many pizza parties in our class. What a celebration! They earned it! I have also been known to bring in donuts, just because they have regularly cooperated with the guest CEOs or successfully completed a lengthy project. But wait, what do you do with a class that gets unacceptable scores?

If a class should choose to get a low score I first must do research as to what happened. I interview students through a written assignment asking them

to explain what went wrong. All students participate in the writing, even if they were absent. They
all write something in class at the same time! I may
meet with groups of students or individually. I do
get to the bottom of the situation. Then I take action from there. Sometimes it might be a letter of
apology from each student in the class to the substitute. It might be phone calls home to parents. It
might be a restriction of the enjoyable activities until
the students understand low scores with a visiting
CEO are not acceptable in the class. In my class a
low score has never been repeated by the same class.

You might question, doesn't giving celebrations
and pizza encourage them to cooperate just so they
will get something? I have considered that perspective. At various times I have been delighted and
surprised with my students response to that concern. Four years ago a pizza celebration occurred
three weeks before the end of the semester. Unexpectedly I had to be absent two more days after the
pizza celebration. How would the students behave?
The pizza celebration was over! There was no further reward for being cooperative two more days.
Yet, when I returned all classes had received A's for
their outstanding behavior. "Why did you chose to
cooperate with the substitute? You already had your
pizza celebration. What was in it for you?" I asked.
As I called on various individuals they gave such
comments as, "We wanted you to be proud of us.
We are mature young adults; we could handle it.
Why not? We had a nice substitute." And some were
even surprised that I would ask such a ridiculous
questions. Since that time it has been clear to me
that the outside rewards, celebrations, and expres-
sions of appreciation move into the hearts of the
students. What comes first? Students have high
regard for themselves and then they cooperate or
they cooperate and then gain high regard for them-

selves. This is an age old self- esteem question. I do not have the answer only experience.

Students really do want to succeed. We must be willing to be tenacious as pit bulls in teaching students misbehavior is not good for them. Incidentally, at the pizza celebration I video tape the students and take pictures. I share these and the previous substitute charts with the next year's class at the beginning of school. This is another way to set the tone for the Great Expectations of the upcoming year.

Show The History of Success

During those first weeks I also show a video of the previous years students. On the tape I have interviewed students and ask what they liked and what was difficult in the class. I include excerpts of fun activities and the pizza celebration for outstanding cooperation with the substitute teachers. Imagine close ups of their favorite pizza. Again, I interview students as to why they are having a pizza celebration. They beam with their mouth full of pizza proclaiming how they chose to cooperate. And the great sacrifice it took to gain those high scores. I ask the students to explain to the camera why I expect everyone to participate as assistants, why I don't allow "I don't know," and any other behaviors I want to reinforce for the incoming class. If you don't know how to video tape this is a skill you need to learn. I purchased our first VCR, television and camera with grant money. I have never been sorry. In fact, when our equipment was destroyed by fire at our school I was at a loss until we were able to purchase replacement equipment with the insurance money. I would never be without a camera in any class I teach. Students enjoy seeing other students perform, they learn from each other, and the tape can be a lasting memory for their family.

Grading: The ScoreCard

The paper work involved in teaching is insurmountable. It never ends. Even with the addition of the computer. There is all that paper work to be graded. Two years ago my husband, a retired high school teacher, was substitute teaching. As he is always discovering new insights and teaching techniques at the high school level I borrow whatever is available and helpful. He suggested a quick grading technique used by Mrs. Hobbs, a high school math teacher, to help me give immediate credit to students for completing their homework. I adapted her idea to my class and call it "The ScoreCard." I am amazed how easy it is. Since I have used it for two years and have had my students evaluate it I can now share it. Incidentally, the students overwhelming loved the idea. I wished I had known about this years ago. What is needed is: a sheet protector for each student, a variety of about 20 rubber stamps of any design, and the actual ScoreCard which you design.

I pass out one sheet protector for each student to last the entire semester and explain all ScoreCards are to remain in their binders. I verbally reinforce the importance of not losing this ScoreCard or any of the ScoreCards to follow. As examples, we discuss papers that parents often need to keep such as a birth certificate, marriage license, contracts, passport, drivers license, and other legal documents. Of course most of those papers can be replaced; however, there is a price to pay: a cost in time and or money. I want to teach the students responsibility.

During the semester I pass out ScoreCards with different assignments. I only give one assignment paper out at a time, collect them and then give out another one. Students fill out the top and include the date received and the due date of the completed, rubber stamped ScoreCard. On one side are listed the Regular Assignments on the other are the Challenge Assignments. Students are expected to complete all the Regular Assignments. Challenge assignments are optional. The scoring is as follows: if the assignment is completed correctly I stamp the area with an upright stamp this equals 5 points. If the assignment is completed, but not as directed, missing parts, late, or does not meet my standards, a stamp is given upside down, this equals 3 points. If the assignments is not completed the square remains empty or an X can be drawn through it. In the following example, if the student completed all the assignments the score would be 45 points.

Name _____   Date Received _____

Period _____   Date Collected _____

Keep this paper as your receipt of credit for your semester grade.

TOTAL POINTS _____

ASSIGNMENT	CHALLENGE
Write a paragraph and explain why you have a contract in this class.	Bring to class a genuine contract and explain its contents to the class.
(Did your parent receive the September newsletter?) Parent signature due 9-22 Parent Signature: 2 stamps	Cut out and paste pictures of 10 people looking at or signing a contract.
Write a list of 53 situations where a contract could be used.	With a partner complete Activity 14 in your textbook. Partners name and signature
Create a contract of your own.	Create a 1 minute dialogue with two people discussing a contract.
Stamped right side up = 5 points Stamped upside down = 3 points	

46

In the next example the total score is 34 points. Each assignment in the square has been clearly explained during the teaching time. The Recorder writes the criteria for the assignment and the due date. If a student completed the assignment, but does not have a ScoreCard, no points are given. I stress over and over the importance of having their ScoreCard in their binders. If they lose the ScoreCard they can get another one; however, I cannot re-stamp all of the assignments they have competed. What is so nice about this system is the little time that it takes and students immediately get feedback as to how they are doing. Also, they can easily see if they need to do the extra challenge assignments. The ScoreCards are easy for all parents to understand. Naturally, parents have been included in the introduction of the ScoreCard and the importance of their children having them in their school supplies.

The typical classroom scene would look like this. I announce that on Wednesday I will be scoring the assignment: *write a list of 53 situations where a contract could be used.* Bring your ScoreCard and the completed assignment. On Wednesday during group or individual work time I am available to see their work and stamp their ScoreCard. It literally takes me seconds to look over their list of *53 situations.* They immediately get a stamp, either straight or upside down. This simple strategy enables me to work with facts. Either they have their assignment completed or they don't. If they forget their ScoreCard or don't do the assignment, I am not angry, hostile, or sarcastic. I just record what I see. It isn't my responsibility to do their work or bring the ScoreCard. Naturally I encourage them to do their best and I do not hesitate to send a copy of their incomplete ScoreCard to their parents. The power and choice rests in the student's hands. The ScoreCard enables the student and parent to see in black and white what is happening or not happening by the choices the students are making.

Name _____ Date Received _____

Period _____ Date Collected _____

Keep this paper as your receipt of credit for your semester grade.

TOTAL POINTS _____

ASSIGNMENT	CHALLENGE
Write a paragraph and explain why you have a contract in this class.	Bring to class a genuine contract and explain its contents to the class.
(Did your parent receive the September newsletter?) Parent signature due 9-22 Parent Signature: 2 stamps	Cut out and paste pictures of 10 people looking at or signing a contract.
Write a list of 53 situations where a contract could be used.	With a partner complete Activity 14 in your textbook. Partners name and signature
Create a contract of your own.	Create a 1 minute dialogue with two people discussing a contract.
Stamped right side up = 5 points Stamped upside down = 3 points	

Be Flexible With Your Students

Imagine, it's a rainy day. The students rubber soled shoes have become wet and upon contact with the tile floor in the classroom there is the most unbelievable squeaking noise. The tardy bell rings and the competition of the squeaky shoes continues. On days like this I turn to the class and say, " Let's get all the squeaking out of our system. Come on everybody squeak those shoes." I join them and we do that for about a minute and then I ask, "Does anybody need more time to squeak their shoes?" If so we continue if not we then go on with the lesson. The point is, eventually they really get tired of squeaking their shoes. I call this being flexible with students. Early in my teaching career I would have never even acknowledged the squeaking noise. I would have scowled at the students until they quieted down. I have learned to acknowledge the obvious.

Another scenario, it's the end of lunch. A girl sobbing walks in the class. She is accompanied by two other girls totally involved in their friend's problem. As I evaluate the situation I can clearly see that the three girls are not ready to participate in the lesson. I inquire as to the problem. "Is she physically hurt, is she in pain?" "No," they respond, "Her boyfriend just broke up with her."

I think to myself, "Her boyfriend? She's had three different boyfriends in the last month. This is not a boyfriend, this is not a relationship. He's more like an acquaintance."

Her supportive friend says, "She really loved him, too."

From my point of view this is ridiculous. "I have an important lesson to contribute to your life." I think. Then I am reminded that until there is some closure on this problem no learning will occur.

"Would you girls like to step out in the hall and help Denise get herself together? I can give you five minutes after that you need to return to class. Can you do that?"

They usually answer yes, and in a matter of moments they return to class. Denise, still clutching her wad of Kleenex and swollen eyes slowly sits down in her seat. The rest of the class looks at her and before the comments begin I say something like, "Students, Denise is having a difficult time right now, but she is going to get better. Since you have all experienced some hard times in your life I know you can understand. She is going to be all right and we need to support her and go on with our lesson.

"Eric, would you get Denise a glass of water, please." Denise may not want or need that glass of water but it gives a chance for the class to get involved in a positive action. It also models helping someone. After that we go on with the lesson.

I might stop near Denise's desk, and quietly say, "You doing OK?"

You may think, "What is the point? I already do that." If you are flexible I applaud you; however, I have observed classes where such situations are not addressed. Sometimes a teacher becomes so preoccupied and inflexible. They blast off like a rocket with their lesson plans in tow ignoring the lack of attention or interest of the class. If you were a student what part of a school day would you remember if this happened to you? The academic lesson or the kindness and understanding of your teacher and someone who gave you a glass of water?

It takes so little to get students back on track. To empower our students we need to build the team work approach. When a student is hurting it can affect the entire project. Students are still accountable and responsible for their work. There may be a delay. They may need more time. They often don't have a history of coping successfully with difficult life situations. They need time. They need our flexible support.

Birdwalk My mother called unexpectedly and told me to meet her at the hospital. Daddy was having an apparent heart attack. I couldn't believe my ears. All my life my mother and dad had been there for me.

"Heart attack is something that happens to really old people, or people I really don't know, but not my beloved dad." I thought. For two weeks dad lingered in the hospital and then slipped into eternity. I returned to school with a broken heart. Many of my colleagues had sent cards, called, sent a beautiful bouquet, and attended the memorial service. My first day back to school my mind was not on nouns or pronouns or acting techniques. I wondered how I would ever go on. When I entered the classroom my students warmly greeted me. Many expressed their concern and sadness at my loss. I noted from the substitute behavior chart that they, as usual, had received 10's. I expressed my gratitude for their support. I asked if they had any questions about my absence. One little boy blurted out, "Mrs. V. said we are not suppose to say anything about death or dying."

I assure him that wasn't the case. They could ask me anything they wanted and I would determine if I wanted to answer the question or not. There were a few relevant questions and then they were ready to continue with our assignment.

I'll never forget at the end of the day Jose walked up to my desk and said, "Dr. Kaiser, you look so sad."

I looked into his warm brown eyes and said, "Jose, I am sad, my heart is breaking because my daddy is gone, but I know in time my heart will heal. Have you ever had a broken heart?"

"Oh, yes, when my grandpa died last year." he responded. "I cried a lot."

"Then you know how I feel, don't you?" It was amazing how free I felt with my students as I proceeded through the grieving process. What helped me to heal, besides my faith, was the support of family, friends, students, and even strangers. In my class caring is a quality I intend to model for my students. Opportunities abound in the classroom where we can support each other. Be flexible when that unexpected situation occurs in your classroom. It may be an invaluable teaching opportunity not listed in the curriculum guide.

T.S. Card

When my husband was a chaplain in the military he would listen and counsel his marines and sailors. On occasion he would have folks who would just come to him to whine about their tale of woe. He got very creative and designed a punch card for those hurting folks. He called it a **Tough Situation Card** or a **T.S. Card.** It had numbers all around it to be punched with the following statement in the middle:

| 1 | 2 | 3 | 4 | 5 | 6 | 7 | 8 | 9 | 10 | 11 | 12 | 13 | 14 |

Tough Situation Card

"Your story has touched my heart! In all my years of military and ministerial experience I have never heard a sadder tale of woe. Unfortunately, your problems defy solutions. In my considered opinion, neither the Red Cross, the Navy Relief, the Legal Officer, nor your Chaplain can offer you any hope for an immediate solution to your dilemma. However, please accept this card as an expression of my sincere sympathy. Bring this card back to be punched whenever you feel in need of more sympathy."

John A Wilson
Chaplain, USNR

I'm sure this card could be adapted to any profession, but with his permission I have adapted a card for teachers who inevitably have students coming to them whining about their lost homework, their lack of sleep, their sore finger, and ad infinitum. What they really want is some attention. This card acknowledges their "tough situation" and humorously provides immediate attention from their teacher.

| 1 | 2 | 3 | 4 | 5 | 6 | 7 | 8 | 9 | 10 | 11 | 12 | 13 | 14 |

Tough Situation Card

Your story has touched my heart! In all my years as a teacher I have never heard a sadder tale of woe. Unfortunately, your problems defy solutions. In my considered opinion, neither the principal, vice principal, the superintendent or the State Department of Education, nor your teacher can offer you any hope for an immediate solution to your problem. However, please accept this card as an expression of my sincere sympathy. Bring this card back to be punched whenever you feel in need of more sympathy.

Dr. Arlene Kaiser
Teacher

On the positive side, students are often anxious to share a story of their recent success. It may or may not relate to school. It may be a huge step of accomplishment and it may be ever so small. Yet they want to be recognized and validated by you for their achievement. This card is an **Celebration and Achievement Card** or a **C.A.A. Card**. This card is a different color than the T.S. Card and allows them to receive recognition when they want it. It also has numbers all around it to be punched with the following positive statement in the middle:

	1 2 3 4 5 6 7 8 9 10 11 12 13 14	

Celebration and Achievement Card

Your story has touched my heart! In all my years of teaching and teacher experience I have never heard a more successful story. Unfortunately, the world is not aware of your great accomplishment. In my considered opinion, the principal, vice principal, the superintendent, the State Department of Education, all your teachers and the entire world should appreciate and celebrate this achievement. Please accept this card as an expression of my admiration. Bring this card back to be punched whenever you feel in need of more acknowledgment, adulation and celebration of your triumphs in life.

Dr. Arlene Kaiser
Teacher

Mrs. Wilson, will you punch my
C.A.A. card?

Do You Remember When You Were This Age?

When was the last time you felt like the age you teach. Perhaps this may seem like a ridiculous question, but have you identified with the feelings and emotions of your students, lately? Unexpectedly a situation occurred which reminded me of the easy embarrassment, frustration, and anger students may feel when pressure is put on them.

A couple of summers ago my family and I visited beautiful Lake Tahoe in California. While we were there, a friend gave us free tickets to see a family magic show at one of the casinos. Now, I am not fond of magic. I have a low tolerance for not understanding how people disappear, how people are sawed in half, or float in the air. Since I don't get the answer I just give up and pretty much eliminate ever seeing a magic show. It only aggravates me. Perhaps you thoroughly enjoy magic shows and that is just fine, but please stay with me. We attended the show and were given front row seats. My family was thrilled to be there and I was "ho hum" about the entire event; however, because of their enthusiasm I attended. The show began with a mime welcoming us and doing magic tricks with scarves and other objects He then came down to the front row and of all people selected me to join him on stage. I did not want to go on stage. Now, I am not afraid of an audience. I enjoy being in front of an audience. I have performed professionally in front of thousands; however, I did not want to go on stage with a mime doing magic. My family, unaware of my perspective on magic, cheered me on and I was center stage with an audience of 2,000 strangers.

The mime proceeded to show me one of his closed hands and then the other closed hand imploring me to guess which hand held the objects. Whichever hand I chose naturally was the wrong one. Throughout the 10 selections of the wrong hand I was uncomfortable, I wanted to return to my seat, in fact leave the show. He kept on and I kept getting the wrong answer to the delight of the audience. Finally, he asked me to pick one last time. Very frustrated I picked the hand and again it was wrong. The audience was now howling. He then pointed to the stage floor behind my back, he guided me to turn around and there were all the objects on the floor. Now this is the important part. As I stared at the objects on the floor the audience roared in laughter. I didn't get the joke. I didn't understand what was going on. My mind was blocked with frustration, anger, embarrassment, and those childhood feelings of appearing stupid. It was only when he returned me to my seat that I understood the situation. As he was having me guess which hand held the object he was throwing them over my head. The audience understood. The mime understood. My family understood. The joke was on me and I didn't like it one bit. Furthermore, I was miserable for the rest of the show. As I wanted to learn from this experience I wondered what I could have done to prevent the entire episode. Also, I had empathy for my students. How many times had I put this kind of pressure on my students? I was reminded of how their minds became shut down and no matter how much I cajoled them they didn't get it. The lesson I learned was not to put my students on the spot and embarrass them. To empathize with them. Let them know that I know that the moment is difficult. That doesn't mean I don't call on them. Sure I do, but I give them an opportunity to get prepared. I tell you, that experience with the mime really put me in touch with my students. I hope you are staying in touch with your own feelings and the feelings of your students in awkward life situations. Interesting how those experience can contribute to our teaching style.

What Do You Want for the Children of This World?

One of the activities I like to do when working with parents or other teachers is ask the question, "What do you want for the children of this world?" We then brainstorm the answers. These are some of the answers I've received throughout the years: compassion, healthy food, getting along with others, family values, respect for others, clean air, spirituality, love and respect for living things, high self-esteem, coping skills, adaptability to change, respect for authority, eagerness to learn, healthy bodies, study skills, perseverance, acceptance of other cultures, assistance to others, caring, sense of humor, ability to read, write and compute . What would you add to the list? In your classroom are there opportunities to learn these attributes from other students? From yourself?

Models for Success

What teachers in your past made a positive impact on your life? I remember two outstanding teachers who have influenced my teaching career. Not long ago I took the opportunity to connect with one of these former teachers. It had been 43 years since I had spoken to my first grade teacher. As I visited my home town for a high school reunion, I was hopeful her name would still appear in the local telephone book. I surveyed the G's and her name leaped out at me as though I had once again been assigned to her class. I excitedly picked up the phone, dialed her number and breathlessly waited. After three rings I recognized her enthusiastic, yet mature voice.

"Miss Gallegan?" I questioned as I slipped back to being a small child. This is Arlene Kaiser. I was in your first grade class. Do you remember me?"

There was silence as she must have been scanning her memory of the hundreds of children she had taught.

"Yes, the one who liked to hula." I rejoiced. After all these years I wanted to call and thank you for the wonderful difference you made in my life. I remember two specific times when you helped me grow through a crisis and another time you touched my heart."

I could sense in her voice that she still understood the trials that first year of school had for a rambunctious child such as me.

"The first time," I continued, "was two week after school started. I was wearing my red ruffled skirt and while playing in the school yard I became horrified as I realized I had forgotten to wear my underpants. I rushed to the classroom sobbing and you gently consoled me and immediately took action to solve my problem. The second memory I have was looking into your smiling face and as a little first grader I would quietly yet boldly say to myself, 'Someday I'm going to marry Miss Gallegan!'

Lastly, I remember becoming engaged to David Rice in first grade. He gave me the most beautiful REAL, plastic, diamond, engagement ring. I was so happy until I lost the ring in the sandbox. Again, I rushed to the classroom sobbing. I was even late from recess. Once again through my sobs you understood my pain. You immediately got someone to watch the class and accompanied me to the sandbox. We searched and searched for my lost treasure. We never did find the engagement ring. But Miss Gallegan, the loss wasn't so great when you shared in my grief."

In high school, Mrs. Bryan modeled successful teaching skills. She was my biology teacher and received respect from students. She was intelligent and loved teaching. She had high standards, high expectations and dressed like a professional. She also had a grand sense of humor. Learning was important, yet she didn't take herself too seriously. We would have lively discussions and then immediately be prompted to switch activities and get back to independent lab experiments. We admired Mrs. Bryan, but most of all we sensed that she really wanted to be our teacher.

How do you create these memories in your classroom? In my classroom, I want students to eagerly come to class ready to start working when the tardy bell rings. They participate in class discussions, individual work, and group work. An atmosphere of mutual respect is evident. It isn't the teacher against the students. Respect, responsibility and trust are the foundation of the classroom. But most of all, in my heart, I want to come to school as a Teacher. I want to look forward to being with my students.

Reprinted by permission, Dave Granlund, Middlesex News, Mass.

Go to the Laboratory:

Every two years I am evaluated by one of the school administrators. I write performance objectives, and assessment techniques for the academic, environmental, and professional areas of teaching. I am evaluated on the planning, organization, and development of the lesson as well as the learning environment I create. From the administrator's point of view I am then given suggestions for improvement and/or generous praise for another successful year of teaching. Having been on both sides of the evaluation process as an administrator and a teacher, I value this process to some degree, however, where is the student input? I am not talking about how they fell about me. But, what is their evaluation? I know many teachers give an end of the year opportunity for students to voice their opinion about their teaching and lesson development. Suggestions are eagerly solicited. I use to do the same evaluation process the last few days of school. At times it was much like having a year book signed with words of praise, being loved, being missed, never to be forgotten, etc. There came a moment of truth in teaching for me where I really wanted to know the truth.

Dr. Stanley Coopersmith, a pioneer in the study and development of self-esteem said that the most important element in the development and enhancement of self-esteem was the child's perception of how valued he was by his parents. Why wouldn't this same concept work in the classroom. What is the child's perception of how I value them? I was sure that they all knew I thought they were terrific. Why, I speak to educators throughout the world about motivating and enhancing student self-esteem, and motivating them to success. Surely, every one of my students would reflect my lectures. Yet in my heart I was troubled. I realized this is a question you don't ask unless you want the answer. One day I asked my students to take out paper and without writing names on it tell me how they thought I felt about them. I wish I could report my perception was on target. Every student knew I valued them and appreciated them regardless of their grades, effort, and talent. That was not the case. I had eight students say that they didn't think I liked them because I hadn't spoken to them in four weeks. Another six students said that they thought I only liked them when they did a good drama assignment. Upon their honest response I saw that I was missing the mark with some of my students. It didn't matter what my perception was, it didn't matter that I bragged in the faculty room about the great rapport I had with students, the truth was staring me in the face. I had some serious homework to do. What is the perception of your students? How do your students think you feel about them? Have you ever asked them? I warn you, this is a question you don't want to ask unless you are ready to take action with the answer.

"Get those old bats out of here!"
NATIONAL ENQUIRER.

Reprinted by permission, Goddard Sherman, National Enquirer

Parent Communication

I typically have approximately 146 -155 students a semester. I realize many other teachers have the same 30-35 students throughout the semester or year. Whatever your count, your students' parents need to be informed as to what is happening in their children's classes. They need communication from you! For years I did not communicate with parents except when their children misbehaved. I was intimidated by parents. I was afraid they would ask a question I couldn't answer, or they would challenge me. Because I am the teacher I was suppose to have all the answers. Fortunately, through years of experience and walking through my fears, I have learned some valuable lessons.

Communicate Regularly With Parents

I did an experiment a few years ago. I made a decision to call every parent in three of my classes during the first three weeks of school. That was about 105 parents. My purpose was to introduce myself and let them know I was looking forward to teaching their children. The mechanics of such a challenge came quite easily. I wrote the following letter:

Teacher
School Address

Dear Parent/Guardian of_____ Period _____

What a privilege and honor to have your child in my Language Arts Class. I have many activities, strategies, and goals for the year. Since Language Arts includes communication skills: writing, reading, speaking, and listening, I thought I would begin the year by communicating with you.

THE BAD NEWS: We have lost our counselors, our class sizes have increased, our library burned, and we are struggling with supplies.

THE GOOD NEWS: I am committed to making this year productive, informative, and enjoyable for your child. I will focus on the academics and include self-esteem building experiences. I want to motivate your child to be healthy, happy, knowledgeable, and a contributing member of our world! After all, in the classroom are the future leaders of our community and country.

I'll be calling you within the next two weeks just to say hello. Don't worry, in order to make 150 calls I must be brief. Please let me know the best time to call you by filling the schedule below. I look forward to talking with you!

Teacher's name

_____
Student's Name   *LA Period*

_____
Parent/Guardian name   *Phone number I should call*

Please pick the best time for me to call you, Monday through Friday
I am teaching 8:45am - 2:15 pm

_____8:00 - 8:30am _____2:30 - 3:30 pm_____7:00 - 9:00pm.

Other_____

_____

REMEMBER: Back to School Night, Wednesday, September 30, 7-8:30pm

I had two students who did not return their letters. One boy said his father could never be reached because of his work schedule. The girl said her mother didn't care. I told them I understood, but to tell their parents I would drive to the place of employment and meet them on their breaks. The next day both students brought in letters with times for me to call their parents. You may ask, "Would you have really gone to their parents work site to meet with them?" Most definitely! I had made a commit-

ment to meet every parent over the telephone, and
if that was not possible I would take the next step.

Birdwalk 🐦   When I was a vice principal in
the junior high school I had a tremendous amount
of contact with parents. The contact with parents
was usually negative. "Your daughter is suspended
for smoking." "Your son was involved in a fight."
"Your daughter has run away from school and we
have notified the police, and your son received a
referral from teacher X for throwing a pencil across
the room." Also there were the meetings where we
gave options to the parent who just found out his/
her daughter was pregnant. The broken dreams, the
heartaches, the frustration and tears of parents were
common to see in my role as an administrator. I have
held their hands, I have cried with them, and even
prayed with them. Through all those situations, I
have never met a parent who did not care. They
may have been tormented by the choices they made,
frustrated with financial burdens, overwhelmed with
responsibility and blemished by their own painful
childhood. They may be repeating the parenting
skills of their own imperfect parents. The cycle goes
on and on. Often times parents said they didn't have
a clue as to their child's problem. Or, they didn't
think they had any choices or help available. I remember those painful times for the parent and the
child. My communication with parents as a teacher
is much more positive than as an administrator. I
have an opportunity to connect with parents before
any serious situation occurs. As a successful
teacher I need the support of parents. We are a team.
Ultimately, we both want the best for their children.
We are in this together. You might be thinking,
"Come on Arlene, haven't you ever had one of <u>those</u>
parents?" Of course I have. I have been misunder-
stood, threatened with dismissal or lawsuits,

belittled in front of a student, and yet I still believe teachers gain parent support through communication. I found that the worst possible response of a parent has been no response: no answered phone calls, no answered letters, or notes. Never forget that the majority of parents in the world are supportive. It is just that small percentage that can often sway our perspective away from the benefits of parent communication.

The time it took to make all those phone calls was about four hours. As stated in the letter, the calls were brief and the parents knew I was calling all parents and granted me just a few minutes. In those few minutes I had made a connection. I was delighted with the majority of the responses. Parents told me I had their support. Parents offered to help with grading papers, chaperoning on field trips, helping in anyway I needed. They also told me of special needs of their child and their own fears about school. It surprised me but many mentioned it was the first time any teacher had ever called just to say hello. The next day in class I could hear the students checking with each other. "Did Dr. Kaiser call your parents?" It was as though the students realized their education was important and I would not hesitate to contact mom or dad or both because we now had a relationship! We were working together for their ultimate good and their teacher was not the enemy.

Speaking to parents on the phone or in person opens the door for communication throughout the semester. During the first two months of school Trisha sat in class and just scowled at me. For some unknown reason I just knew she hated the class and hated me. Her body language, her vocal tone, and the rolling of her eyes upward really discouraged me. I couldn't imagine what I had done or what had happened in class to cause her such agitation. One day while grocery shopping in the produce department her mother recognized me. Before I could raise my concern and ask about Trisha her mother began to rave about my class and how Trisha just loved it. "Every day we hear about Dr. Kaiser's class. She just thinks you're wonderful." "Wonderful?" I thought. "Why doesn't someone tell Trisha's face?" As the semester progressed I got to know Trisha and indeed that was just Trisha. If I hadn't been approachable to Trisha's mom via the phone call I might have persisted in my perception of Trisha throughout the semester.

Newsletters

Another colleague, Sherry Blackman, showed me the value of writing a brief newsletter for the parents each month. It is a one or two sided page and tells what is going on in class. I usually write it on the computer with a very simple program such as *The Writing Center*. If I couldn't create it on the computer I would write the copy and give the assignment to one of my computer literate students. Since my students are cooperative I always salute them with praise in the newsletter. That is also an incentive for the newsletters to get home. Who wants to take home bad news? I require a signature on a ScoreCard or homework book to indicate the parents have received the newsletter.

Sending Letters Home

I send very few letters through the mail. Usually a student will take the note home or I will call a parent. But have you ever sent important letters home through the mail to the students' parents only to find out that it had been intercepted by the student and the parents never did receive the letter? I have not knowingly had this happen to me, but another strategy shared by my colleague Cheryl S., a high school teacher, intrigued me. If you are concerned that the sight of the return address of the school on the envelope will delete your effort to contact the parent do this: in your own mail keep all the return envelopes you receive from the phone company, gas company, insurance, medical facilities, etc. The next time you need to send a letter to the students parents send it in one of those envelopes. You should include a letter that states something to the fact that: Dear Parent: I am Billy's English teacher and I knew if I sent this letter to you in this envelope you would be sure to receive it as it concerns the following vital information....Billy is failing English. He has not turned in 22 assignments...etc. It is a shame we have to resort to such methods, but sometimes we must do what works to keep the parents informed. I also look at it as another way we can recycle envelopes.

Give Parents the Opportunity to Help

It was the start of school and the door stop connected to the outside door of the classroom was broken. Every time I opened the door to circulate air in the warm classroom it wouldn't stay open. Five periods a day I struggled with that door stop. I knew I could send in a work order to the district's maintenance crew, but with their overworked scheduled my simple need might slip to the end of the list. I included a plea for help in one of the newsletters and the following day a father came to school with a hammer and a new door stop. In a matter of minutes the problem was solved. I was so grateful to that father and his daughter witnessed him helping a desperate teacher. Another time a window blind, which I used as background for video taping, became completely tangled and unusable. Again, a plea for help via the newsletter. Both parents of one of my students came to remove it and work on it over the weekend. We all cheered when it was returned and we could use that back drop again.

Test the Waters

Three years ago I phoned a mother because her daughter had participated in an activity that had completely broken my trust. Trust and responsibility are to be demonstrated in my classroom. I thought the inappropriate activity warranted a quick phone call to mom. Upon hearing her hello, I identified myself and explained the situation. Well, this parent went totally out of control. She swore at me, screamed at me, told me that I had no business humiliating her daughter and she would be calling the principal and ultimately the superintendent. Through her monologue of ranting and raving I was in shock which was followed by anger. I thought to myself, "I don't have to take this abuse. I don't get paid enough money to be treated like this!" Which was followed by thoughts of, "I'm a professional. There is something more going on here. Just ride this out and more will be revealed." When the mother slammed the phone down in my ear I was near tears. I didn't sleep too well that night, and arrived at school early to see the vice principal. In our conversation he provided insight to the situation. This mother had just discovered that her boyfriend had been molesting her daughter, my student, for a number of years. She was guilt ridden that this horrible incident has occurred. I was the receiver of her pent-up hostility. I was at the wrong place at the wrong time.

Times have changed. It is not like twenty or more years ago where we could assume parents were automatically supportive of us. Because of that incident, I have learned to test the waters. Whenever I contact a parent I question if this is a good time to talk and state that I have some concerns about their child. I gently prod to see if circumstances have changed at home, or if there is some information I should know about their child. In most cases, the parents are ready to talk and have no hidden agenda. Still, it is wise to test the waters.

Parents are an important part of the educational process. They have helped with field trips, casting plays and serving refreshments for celebration days. The elementary teachers are wonderful at using parent support. It seems when students advance to the middle school and high school parents get the impression they are not needed. Also, their teenagers inform them they are not wanted at the secondary school. We do a disservice to exclude parents.

Questions and Answers

What do you do with the student who monopolizes the class with questions or comments?

It is not uncommon to have an eager student participant in your class. They are constantly waving their hands to answer any question you pose. Or, even before you have finished your instructions up flies the hand which totally distracts you. Whenever I have a student who matches this profile, I speak to him/her alone. I tell him/her I admire the courage and exuberance of their participation in class; however, at times he/she does distract me. I want to give other students an opportunity to participate, therefore, I will allow them two opportunities during the period to either ask a question or give an answer. Inevitably, I will say, "You've had other teachers tell you this too haven't you." And they respond, "Yes, in fifth grade or last year." The challenge for the teacher is to be consistent. When that hand flies up, remember to say, "Is this one of the questions you want to use. Often then say, Oops, no, I'll wait." This simple techniques really works and helps the student to appraise the situation and exert some self-control.

What do you do with the students who aren't doing anything? They just sit there and do nothing. They don't participate. They are not a behavior problem; they just choose to do nothing.

John was such a student. He did nothing! First I reviewed his cum folder, for insight as to his past history to see if there was a pattern. More often than not there is a history including a lack of motivation, or sometimes a sudden, negative shift in performance. In John's case he had shown a lack of motivation since fourth grade. Up until that time he had been an A student. There was no indication of any special needs. He was capable of doing the work. I met with John privately. He was surprised that he was failing, in spite of notices to him and to his parents, he was unbelievably surprised. I alerted him to the great possibility that he would ultimately fail the semester unless he chose a different course of action. I asked how he was doing in his other classes. He replied, "Fine!" After discussion with the other teachers, I discovered he was failing two more classes! I contacted his parents again and encouraged them to arrange for a conference with all of his teachers at the same time. The conference was called. We each gave input and created a contract with his input. The conference was over and agreement was made he would concentrate on completing his homework. His parents were supportive and it seemed John was on the way to improvement. However, after two weeks of constant reminders, notes home, and phone calls John had not made any effort to follow the contract. I was understanding, I was firm, I was helpful, I was available. Still no improvement. I was giving John most of my energy. Everything we tried as a team failed. In desperation I tried another tactic. Without great emotion I told John that it was clear that he had chosen to fail. I would respect his decision therefore, I was going to give him a new contract, a Failure Contract. The contract stated that he would not participate in class. He would not turn in homework. He would just sit in the back of the room and do nothing. In turn, I would not hassle him about work. He would receive a failing grade for the entire semester. This contract was immediately put into effect for two weeks. After the two weeks he could decide if he wanted to continue the contract or write a new one for success. He signed the contact, I signed the contract, and after a long discussion with his parents they sighed the contract. This was only for my class. Naturally he bragged to the other students about his special contract and the following Monday I explained to the class that John had chosen to not participate in class for the next two weeks and perhaps the rest of the semester at a great cost. If they had any further questions about the great cost they would need to talk to John. That was it. From that point on I treated John as if he didn't exist. I was polite, kind, but expressed little emotion. Whenever he would start to get involved with other students I reminded him he needed to get back to the work of doing nothing at his desk. After the first week I could tell that he was very uncomfortable. He wanted to interact with his friends. He was not getting any attention from me. I was not even hassling him. At the end of the two weeks I calmly called him to my desk to make a decision. We were starting a new class project and we would be working in groups. Did he want to participate or return to his contract. He stated that he wanted to participate. I told him to write a new contact and submit it to me with a description of what he was willing to do. I firmly informed him that his participation would effect his failing grade. That if he wanted to fail this was not the way to go. I could tell he was absolutely bewildered by my response. It seemed that the more I let go the more he chose a course of responsible action. John did pass the class with a C. Periodically I checked in with him to see if he wanted to return to the old one. I carefully planned my actions so that I would be perceived as very calm and matter of fact. After all, his choice was about his life. In retrospect I remember that this unorthodox approach gave me peace of mind and put the responsibility where it should have been...back to the student. This is an approach I would use selectively. The parents and the school administration must be included.

What do you do with the student who regularly misbehaves?

Since all my students sign a contract I have some direction. I immediately contact the parents. My experience has been that I have never met a parent that didn't care. I have met parents who have been frustrated with their own lives, parents who were struggling to make ends meet, parents besieged by the school about behavior problems with their children, parents angry with the school system because we can't fix their child. Parents who should have never been parents! Still, they have cared about their children. Not the way you and I might care, but still they cared!

First, I keep in contact with parents. Most of my students' parents live in a twenty mile radius of the school. Some work miles away. I will usually telephone in the evening and never after 9:00 P.M. If I never get a response, I will make a home or work visit. I send a notice to the parents that I will be stopping by their home or worksites to meet with them. In 98% of the notices I have sent home I get a call that they would prefer to meet with me at school. All of the meetings with parents include their child. After the initial conference we may meet privately. The student already knows what is going on. I don't want to perpetuate any secretive agendas. I explain to the student and parents what specifically is the problem. I also want to know how the student perceives me. Is there something I have done to offend the student. Is this a personal attack or misdirected anger. In this conference I know I can't solve a history of misbehavior. I just don't want it demonstrated in the classroom!

Birdwalk Haven't you had students who had a reputation as terrors in the school, and yet cooperated in your classroom? I have had some of the school's top ten behavior problems but in my class they were productive. They cooperated. So, I come from a point of view that just because they hate school, hate teachers, hate life, and are prepared to take over the class, I will not tolerate a student destroying my class. I earned the right to teach. Didn't you? I took all those classes, researched and wrote all those papers. I took exciting classes with energetic teachers and boring classes with the most unmotivated educators I ever met. I have experienced life up to my present age. I have a long, valuable history. I have lessons I have learned about life. I have information to share. For those difficult students assigned to my class: I will give them respect as a human being, I will not deliberately embarrass them, I will not manipulate them to the point where they will exploded in anger. They may choose to fail the subject I teach, but they will still learn about life from just being in my class. I will **not** let them destroy my love for teaching or my responsibility to teach effectively!

We then end the conference with an understanding of what is not acceptable in my class. Together we create a new individualized contract with consequences clearly defined. The consequences will range from: a verbal warning, time out, a call home, a parent or guardian to attend class with the student, class suspension, and lastly school referral. During the last five years I have had a total of five classroom suspensions. Only with intolerable situations do I involve school administration. Usually I get administrative support and I think this is because I send in so few referrals. When I call for help I need support. Ten years ago I demanded to file a police report on a particular student. The student appeared to have serious psychological problems and yet looked like an angel. I did this to alert "the system" that psychologically this child needed help. Needless to say, my insistence was not well received, but it did get action. Hopefully, this student eventually received professional help. If he didn't, I expect to see his name in the headline news involved in a serious crime.

Birdwalk Denise was sent to my office when I was a vice principal. She was an eighth grader who had a vendetta for all female teachers. She was disrespectful, belligerent, and defiant. Her choice of behaviors resulted in continuous suspensions. With her male teachers, she was no problem. After meeting with her stepmother, I was impressed with her devotion to her stepdaughter. She had a full time job, yet took time from work to attend the conference. It was clear that she was willing to do anything to remedy the situation.

With Denise present we decided that the next time she chose to be disrespectful to a teacher, Denise would be suspended for the day and the following day her stepmother would accompany

Denise to all of her classes. She would ride the bus and eat lunch with her stepdaughter's friends. Stepmother was willing to take time off from work to do this for up to a week. Now Denise was not convinced in the lest that Stepmother would really take time off. I must admit I had my doubts was well. As you would expect Denise once again got sent to the office. I immediately followed our agreement called stepmom and made arrangements for her to attend school with her stepdaughter. Denise listened to my call and smirked that her stepmother wouldn't be coming the next day. After alerting all the teachers and making arrangements with the school bus I wondered if the stepmother would go through with her promise. Sure enough, the next day I greeted the bus and there stood Stepmom wearing the cutest outfit. To the humiliation of Denise, she looked more like an eighth grader than a stepmom. She walked the halls with Denise, she attended all her classes with Denise, she hung around with Denise and her friends and even ate lunch with Denise. This was all just too much! At the end of the day I met with Denise and Stepmom and asked if Stepmom would like to come back the next day as Mrs. Betts would be conducting an exciting science experiment. Denise assured me her stepmom would not need to come back. The following day Denise proved herself and we never had another incident. To this day I will never forget the love and dedication Denise's stepmom had for her stepdaughter. She was an authentic model of parent dedication!

Another situation didn't turn out so well. Ben was a seventh grader well liked by his peers and teachers. He wasn't academically motivated yet squeezed by with passing grades. As vice principal I had been privy to information that he might be involved in drugs. Not Ben, I thought. He was one of my favorites to see on campus and especially during my daily lunch duty. One day he was brought in by the counselor for selling marijuana. After a search the evidence was found and he admitted to selling it regularly to the other students. The legal steps were taken, the police were contacted and I requested that he be picked up at lunch time. He was handcuffed and lead out to the police car with a majority of the students watching during lunch. I intended that to happen. The other students saw the consequence of drug involvement. Ben was expelled for a year. His mother and I wept and at her request we prayed together. It broke my heart to see Ben leave our school. I don't know what ultimately happened to Ben. That day of Ben's arrest, I'm hopeful many students made a recommitment to a drug free lifestyle. Drug addiction eventually culminates in sorrow, regret, physical pain, hospitalization, institutionalization, and/or death. There is nothing glamorous about drugs. Some educators may disagree with my decision to openly display Ben's arrest, but if it made an impression on one child, it was a wise choice.

I have been in schools where I couldn't believe the deplorable condition of the school, the lack of supplies and where teaching moral was at an all time low. I have been in other schools where it reminded me of a prosperous corporation with state of the art technology and enthusiastic teachers. I have walked the halls of schools during passing time where I have felt extremely uncomfortable and other schools where I felt as though I was in a country club atmosphere. You probably work in one of the two or somewhere in the middle. I work in a school somewhere in the middle. I still have those teaching nightmares before the start of school. I hear rumors about an upcoming class or specific individuals who have caused serious problems for another school or teacher and I hope those students aren't in my class. I still struggle with classes where students are not on the same level of knowledge and learning. How can I reach them all? I still ache for the student who has a deplorable home life and yet still has a glimmer of a dream of becoming a professional football player. How do I realistically encourage him but not kill his dream? What can I do with the student who is completely turned off to school? Or the parents who act as though they don't care. What about the student who shows all the signs of gang involvement and/or promiscuity?

Polishing the Diamond

How is our world to continue if these children and young adults are not inspired, taught, and empowered? Who will help them? Who will make that important difference in their lives? You will. The students that I didn't reach, the students that didn't grasp the lessons I taught, the students that were not ready to learn "the lesson," will be inherited by you. You will make the difference! You will take that teachable moment in your hands and create astounding discoveries for the student to grasp. And the student will be ready to learn from you! Ready to learn the lessons I missed. Ready to hear your message.

It's like polishing a diamond. I polish just one facet and sometimes it doesn't look as if I am making any progress. Then the unfinished diamond is passed onto you and you polish another facet, one teacher to another it is passed, until one day it is a beautiful multifaceted diamond that dazzles all who see it. But remember, no one person was responsible for the polishing of that diamond.

In the same way I am not responsible for all of the child's education. Students will come to your class and you will contribute to their lives. You will pass them on to another teacher and another. Ultimately these students will enhance our world. Aren't you relieved to know that it isn't all up to you? We all share in the responsibility of polishing that diamond and we <u>do</u> make a difference. Happy teaching!